NEW YORK CITY

CAPITAL OF THE WORLD

FINANCE CAPITAL
MEDICAL CAPITAL
FASHION CAPITAL
MEDIA CAPITAL

CAPITAL OF THE WORLD

A world leader, the city of New York is the center for health care, finance, banking, technology, communication, design, architecture, and almost any sphere one can think of. Hence making New York the most powerful, resourceful, and resilient city in the world.

NEW YORK CITY

CAPITAL OF THE WORLD

To...... Joel Cohen ....

From..... Balik Khayan ....

Date.... January 24. 2020 ....

Place..... Met @ NYC & Co. Function

Note..... Please call me ....
....
I need your help ....
....

Printed in the United States of America

Copyright ©2019 by the Morgan Publishing House Inc. All rights reserved.

MORGAN PUBLISHING HOUSE INC.
— Est. 1998 —

Visit us at: www.morganpublishinghouse.com
Contact us at: babu@morganpublishing.us

Once Is Not Enough!

It is impossible to take in all that New York has to offer in one single visit. Blessed with diversity, varied economic status, sports, arts, finance, and culture, the only melting pot of the whole world is New York!

This ever-changing "city that never sleeps" offers a taste of almost everything from multi-cuisine palette to bar hopping, sightseeing, cruising, and much more.

With over 60 million annual visitors, it is fair to say that, when it comes to New York,

Once Is Never Enough!

"Different as our lives are, we are bound together by an invisible thread.
We are united by the profound and powerful fact that we are all New Yorkers."

- Bill de Blasio
Mayor of New York

Preface

The book is a tribute to the City of New York, which has given wings to every dreamer, stood up to the test of time, balanced the old and the new, making it a multicultural mix of both quirk as well as intelligence.

"New York City: Capital of the World" is what every New Yorker as well as anyone in the world who has visited or is visiting the City would relate and remember New York for. It is a day-to-day factual, informative, and concise explanation as to what the City has to offer, why is it one of the favorite tourist destinations, and how it lives up to every word of being a true "melting pot."

"The City" or as it is often referred to "The Big Apple" has been the hotspot for almost every industry an economy can wish for. Calling to gather the think tank from world over whether it be medical, engineering, sports, or arts. The one thread that binds these brains together is the fact that they are all a living proof to the pulse and the capacity that this City delivers.

As the book traces a glimpse of the historical events and the rise of the Big Apple it shows the five boroughs and portrays a complete picture of the rise of this

Empire State.

. . . All men are created equal, that they are endowed by their Creator with certain unalienable Rights, that among these are Life, Liberty and the Pursuit of Happiness . . .

The United States Declaration of Independence

I pledge allegiance to the flag of the United States of America, and to the republic for which it stands, one nation under God, indivisible, with liberty and justice for all.

" . . . this nation, under God, shall have a new birth of freedom—and that government of the people, by the people, for the people, shall not perish from the earth. "

—Abraham Lincoln
16th President of the United States of America

Since time immemorial, people from all over the world have come to this "city of dreams" to be a part of this "New World" full of opportunities and plenty,

resulting in a city that is rich in every possible field and a true example of how a harmonious diversity can become a global power.

From the 1850s this great city welcomed immigrants from Europe, Africa, Asia, South America, and gradually Australia to build this city of immigrants, forming a thousand success stories for generations to tell and live in.

For every person who entered this place it was all about the American dream and most of them are living proof to how much the Empire State gives back to those who dare!

The City of Dreams

Make your wishes come true!

Looking at New York City now, it's hard to imagine that this island was once a remote wilderness carpeted by lush green forests, woods, and streams. Where now rise skyscrapers hundreds of stories high, there once grew trees of pine, oak, maple, sweet gum, cedar, basswood, and hawthorn.

Instead of structured roadways laid out in a neatly patterned grid, there was once an undulating and verdant topography filled with hills and gullies left exposed after the last glacial recession 10,000 years ago.

This rich green habitat was once the home of diverse wildlife. Leopards, deer, wolves, and frogs thrived.

In the 16th century, there also dwelt here the Lenape, a Native American tribe. They called the island "Manahatta," meaning "hilly island," and they farmed portions of the land and canoed the river to fish and trade with other Native American tribes living along the banks of River Hudson (called Shatumec back then).

But soon, sails began to appear on the horizon, signaling the start of a long influx of foreigners into this fertile, bountiful land. These explorers would return home with stories, prompting their governments to send them back with missions for further explorations.

continued on page 24

"Give me your tired, your poor, your huddled masses yearning to breathe free . . . "

—Emma Lazarus

As people watched in wonder, Lady Liberty stood three hundred and five feet tall and came to life on October 28th, 1886, as "Liberty Enlightening the World." This grand statue was a gift from France to the people of America as a universal symbol of freedom and democracy as both nations were allies during the American Revolution.

Those who bravely overcame governmental obstruction, religious persecution, and traveling through rough waters for days heaved a sigh of relief and joy at the sight of the statue greeting them in the land of the free and brave.

✈ **AIRPORTS**

1. J.F. Kennedy International Airport
2. La Guardia Airport
3. Newark Liberty International Airport
4. Teterboro Airport
5. New York Stewart International Airport
6. Westchester County Airport

🚁 **HELIPORTS**

7. TSS Heliport
8. Blade Lounge Wall St.
9. Air Pegasus
10. Downtown Manhattan Heliport

SEAPLANE

11. Skyport Seaplane

🌉 **BRIDGES**

12. Throgs Neck Bridge
13. Whitestone Bridge
14. R.F.K. Bridge
15. Queensboro Bridge
16. Williamsburg Bridge
17. Manhattan Bridge
18. Brooklyn Bridge
19. Verrazzano Bridge
20. Goethals Bridge
21. G.W. Bridge

TUNNELS

22. Midtown Tunnel
23. Hugh Carey Tunnel
24. Holland Tunnel
25. Lincoln Tunnel

PLACES

26. Broadway
27. Fifth Ave
28. Central Park
29. 57th Street
30. 42nd Street
31. Theater District
32. Times Square
33. Diamond District
34. UN Headquarters
35. 34th Street
36. Port Authority
37. Garment District
38. Fashion Ave
39. Penn Station
40. Bryant Park
41. Empire State Building
42. Greenwich Village
43. SOHO
44. Chinatown
45. Financial District
46. Statue of Liberty
47. North Cove Ferry
48. Pier A Ferry
49. South Ferry
50. Ferry to Governors Island
51. Wall Street
52. One World Trade Center
53. Governor's Island
54. Water Taxi Ⓦ

FINANCIAL
CAPITAL

The "Fearless Girl" statue stares defiantly at the "Charging Bull." It was installed to promote gender equality and women's employment in leadership roles.

New York City is considered the most competitive city in the world because of its ability to continuously attract world-class businesses, making it indisputably the financial capital of the world.

Home to two of the world's largest stock exchanges—the New York Stock Exchange (NYSE) and the NASDAQ—the city also headquarters 45 of the fortune 500 companies.

Boasting an unparalleled banking sector, New York City is home to 160 banks from over 40 different countries. The Big Apple's financial service industry provides wages to over 60 percent of the city's private sector. It is estimated that the city has over 700,000 jobs in hospitality, law, accounting, and technology primarily because of Wall Street.

Did you know that Times Square is so brightly lit you can actually see it from outer space?

Glittering and shining all night long, Times Square is famous for its majestic billboards and advertisements that attract millions of people from all walks of life. Lighting up Broadway, this intersection is often referred to as the "crossroads of the world." Famous for its New Year Eve's ball drop ceremony, millions of people squeeze shoulder-to-shoulder in Times Square to welcome the New Year with panache!

CROSSROADS OF THE WORLD

The iconic 42nd Street teems with the world's most famous theaters, cinemas, all-night shopping centers, sports bars, and rooftop restaurants packed together from the Hudson to the East River.

The grandly designed Grand Central Terminal is one of the busiest train stations in the world. Renowned for its striking architecture and abundance of shopping and dining facilities it is a one of a kind station, not to be missed.

The first people to actually settle here, however, were the Dutch, led by an Englishman named Henry Hudson in a boat called the **Half Moon**.

They arrived in a group of 30 families and settled down on Nutten Island in 1624, now renamed Governor's Island. Two years later, the settlement moved to spread along the southern tip of Manhattan. The story goes that Peter Minuit, the Dutch colonial governor, purchased the island from the Lenape for the mere sum of twenty-four dollars in trade goods.

Historians emphasize, however, that the Native Americans thought of this transaction as merely a promise to peacefully share the land with the Dutch. They never meant it to be a direct handover.

So in these circumstances, New Amsterdam was born, named after the capital of the Netherlands.

It rapidly grew into a busy, free trade port dealing with the sale and trade of fur, slaves, grains, and other goods. One of the most precious currencies was beaver fur that was exported throughout Europe, and the demand was so high that beavers were nearly driven to extinction.

As more and more traders poured in, they raised the mix of ethnicities and races, and soon, the settlement included nationals from lands as diverse as England, Ireland, France, Sweden, Germany, Asia, Brazil, the West Indies, and more.

continued on page 36

NEW YORK CITY
since 1664
HISTORY

The city
that never sleeps

Dining by the river

From Greenwich Village to Chelsea, from Brooklyn to the Upper West Side, there is a never-ending wonderland of fabulous foods to be tasted and memorable fun to be had! Numerous restaurants dotting the waterfront offer a taste of various cuisines. Visitors munch on delicacies while lazing around, soaking up the sun and enjoying the experience of a lifetime.

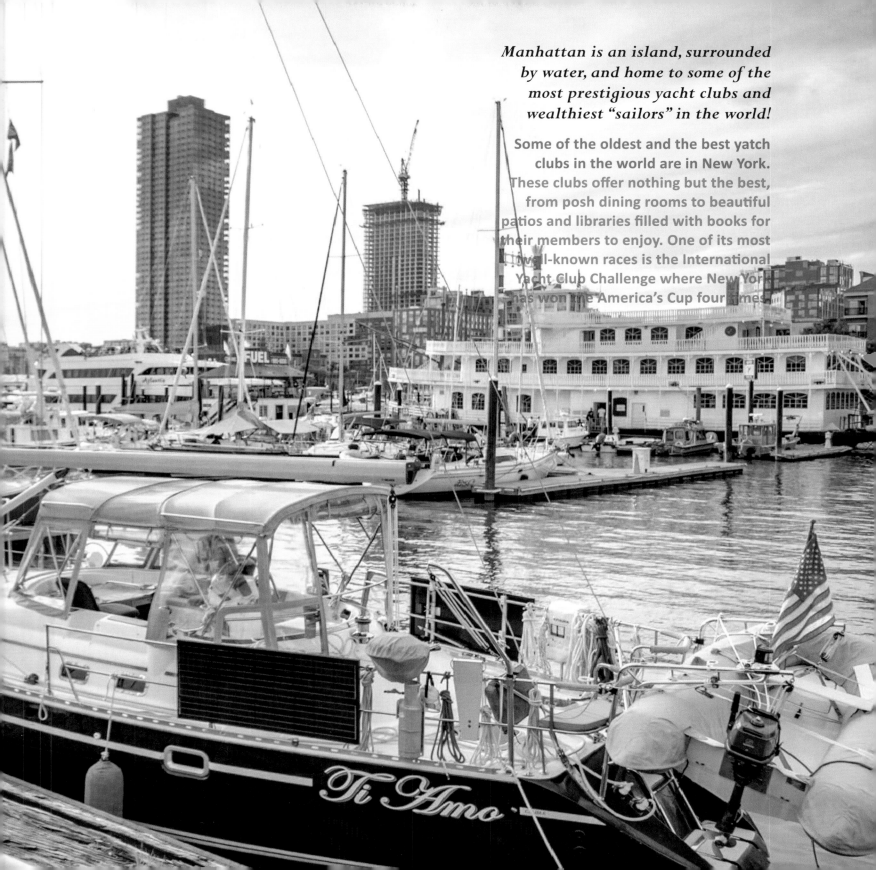

Manhattan is an island, surrounded by water, and home to some of the most prestigious yacht clubs and wealthiest "sailors" in the world!

Some of the oldest and the best yatch clubs in the world are in New York. These clubs offer nothing but the best, from posh dining rooms to beautiful patios and libraries filled with books for their members to enjoy. One of its most well-known races is the International Yacht Club Challenge where New York has won the America's Cup four times.

You are bound to be serenaded no matter where you are in New York City

If you are a music lover, New York is the place to be with a variety of choices including jazz, cabaret, concerts, subway musicians, and of course, Broadway! Some of the most unique and eclectic musicians head to the subway to practice their many talents including percussion, guitar, dancing, and horns!

Empire State Building

Completed in 1931, the iconic Empire State Building stands 102 stories high and was the world's tallest skyscraper for nearly 40 years.
The site is so popular among young men who desire to propose romantically that the management launched annual Valentine's wedding events on the 86th floor.

*The skyscraper is also home to the annual Run-Up event, where hundreds of athletes from around the world race a total of 1,576 steps from the lobby to the 86th-floor Observatory.
This landmark building is one of Big Apple's main attractions, with millions of visitors every year!*

New York City is proudly diverse with thousands of places of worship including churches, Buddhist temples, mosques, Hindu temples, and synagogues. In fact, there are now six thousand churches within the city, one thousand synagogues, and one hundred mosques serving the people of NYC.

Places of worship

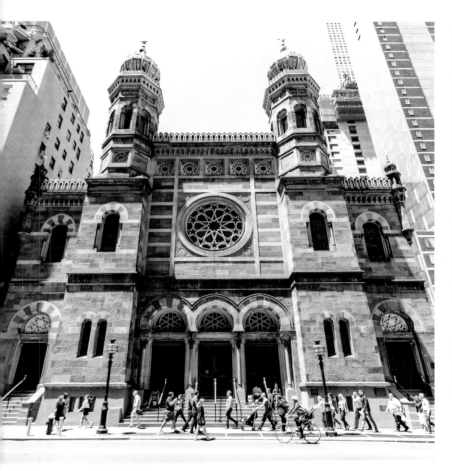

One of the oldest synagogues within the city is the Central Synangogue on Lexington Ave. However, the most iconic place of worship in New York would be St. Patrick's Cathedral on Fifth Ave. Representing the Hindu faith is the Ganesh Temple in Flushing.
Other popular religious attractions are the Mahayana Buddhist Temple, the Eldridge Street Synagogue, and the Islamic Cultural Mosque on Third Ave.

Whether attending for worship or for the beauty and architecture, New York City is home to many of the most sacred places of worship you'll ever have the joy of visiting!

Each fall, for a week in September, the UN headquarters in this international territory is abuzz with activity as leaders from across the world are in the city to attend the General Assembly. The mission of the UN is to support peace and security around the world and advance human rights, education, and health while promoting countries' economies and safeguarding the environment. Therefore, this is a key global annual event where leaders have the opportunity to address the world and speak of their concerns.

The impressive complex making up the United Nations, overlooking the East River, stands proudly as a beacon of peace and prosperity for all.

This beautiful eighteen acres of land was generously donated by the Rockefeller family, and treasured to this day by those who value human life and freedom for all.

On June 26th, 1945, fifty countries were represented in the United States, making world history as they signed the Charter of the United Nations, officially forming this organization at Lake Success, New York. Now 193 magnificent flags lining the UN headquarters stir in the breeze, as all the colors add testament to the commitment of these member countries to promote the rights and well-being of its people.

New York is simply the greatest city in the world!

With over eight million people in the Big Apple and more than 20 million people in the greater New York area, **it is both the most populous and the largest metropolitan area in the United States.**

Forests and meadows were cleared out and planted as farms, known as boweries. Back when New Amsterdam was established, the original city it was named after, was considered one of the most liberal centers of the world. According to the historian, Rusell Shorto, this factor contributed significantly to the shaping of present-day New York City into the cultural and cosmopolitan center it is now.

With the explosive growth of New Amsterdam, there also broke out conflicts between the new settlers and the natives. A semblance of government began to appear as Willem Kieft—the director of New Amsterdam—began to hold weekly meetings overseen by his law enforcement officer.

In 1653, New Amsterdam finally adopted a municipal charter under the leadership of Peter Stuyvesant, and work was started on a fort. But the fort was of poor construction.

When the English arrived with their navy, they seized control of the city from the Dutch and renamed it New York, after the Duke of York, who was the man responsible for sending soldiers to conquer New Amsterdam.

As the British extended their dominion across the country, New York became a major port, growing rapidly in population and diversity.

continued on page 50

POWERING AMERICA'S ENGINE

Thanks to its ceaseless supply of power, the city is able to play host to its massive, breathtaking industries, while it dazzles and sparkles beautifully to keep the $2 trillion+ economy rolling.

A mega-grid of power generation fuels the gigantic machinery of New York City. The city needs a powerhouse supply of robust and reliable electricity generation all year round. Over 200 companies, including some of the strongest players like ConEd, plug their resources into this grid to keep it throbbing with power. Large investments are being made toward wind farming and solar power for more renewable and eco-friendly power supplies in the years to come.

ONE WORLD TRADE CENTER

The new and iconic One World Trade Center in Lower Manhattan is the tallest building in the Western Hemisphere.

Standing tall above the city with the most striking views of Manhattan is One World Observatory on the 102nd floor. The remarkable sights and the forest of skyscrapers mesmerize New Yorkers and tourists alike.

Many industry leaders have made One World Trade home due to its innovative architecture, grand open spaces, and its pulsing energy.

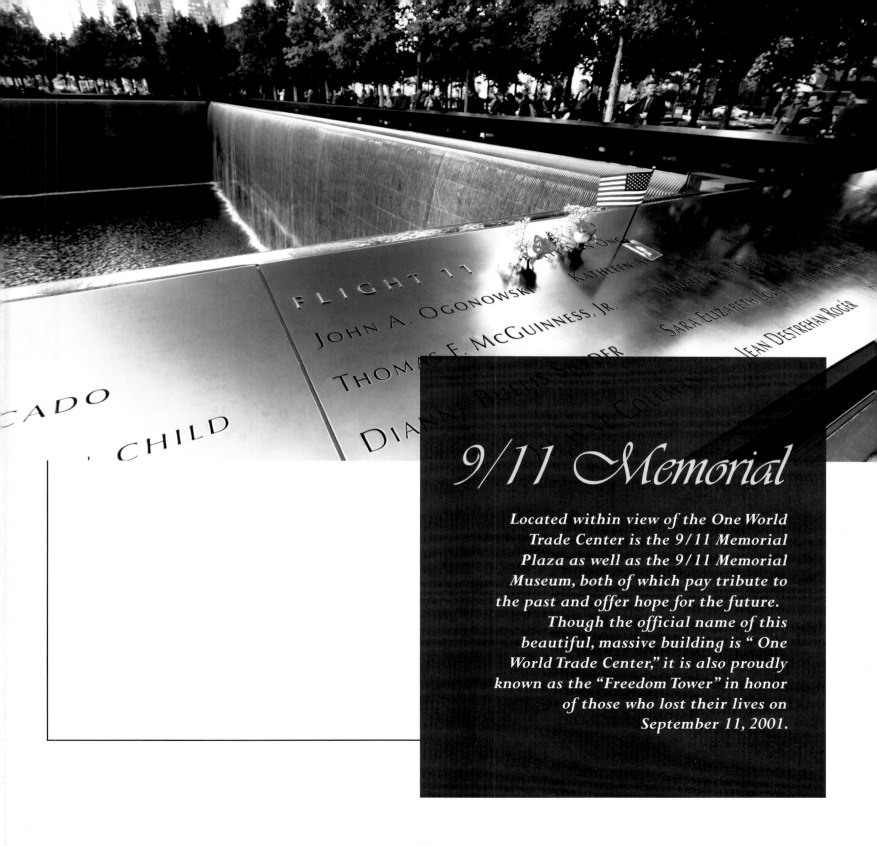

9/11 Memorial

Located within view of the One World Trade Center is the 9/11 Memorial Plaza as well as the 9/11 Memorial Museum, both of which pay tribute to the past and offer hope for the future. Though the official name of this beautiful, massive building is " One World Trade Center," it is also proudly known as the "Freedom Tower" in honor of those who lost their lives on September 11, 2001.

Winter season in the Big Apple

The sight of Central Park covered in snow is one that visitors never forget. The Bryant Park Winter Village is adorned with eye-candy kiosks and eateries galore, while the outdoor rink is filled with hot cocoa and winter treats.

New Yorkers are most fond of the winter months as they flock to enjoy this cold weather with ice-skating rinks, holiday festivals, Rockefeller Center's Christmas tree lighting, and the famous Times Square Ball drop on New Year's Eve. There is no shortage of activities both indoors and out when it comes to the city's winter.

There are cozy restaurants and bistros to enjoy on virtually every corner before or after an evening at a comedy club, cabaret, or Broadway show! So, bundle up for winter fun in New York City and explore the "winter wonderland!"

New York City is on a hot streak when it comes to tourism, breaking records for the past eight years and bringing more than sixty million visitors in 2017 alone!

Because of the hundreds of unique neighborhoods to explore and the vibrant and ever-evolving happenings in every corner of our city, the Big Apple continues to attract millions both domestically and international, generating billions of dollars per year for the New York economy. With countless attractions that New York has to offer, including its historic landmarks, museums, parks, restaurants, and shows,

the economy of the greatest city continues to grow as it opens its arms worldwide to visitors each and every year!

ONCE IS NOT ENOUGH

Manhattan

One of the most popular attractions in all of New York City is the iconic Rockefeller Center in the heart of Midtown Manhattan. This Art Deco landmark spanning 22 acres and featuring 19 commercial buildings is a year-round New York destination and home to numerous events including the lighting of the famous Rockefeller Center Christmas tree, which is broadcast live on television around the world each year!

Home to NBC Studios as well as Saturday Night Live, Rockefeller Center is a haven for tourists who'd like the opportunity to participate in the audience or go backstage and behind the scenes of some of the most popular television shows in history!

Thanksgiving Day Parade

There are many ways to celebrate Thanksgiving in New York City in the month of November, but one of the most cherished events is the Macy's Thanksgiving Day Parade!

Thanksgiving Day is also a time for just that: giving thanks together as a family sharing a turkey meal for all the blessings received in life while giving respect and gratitude to all who made our lives that much better!

The New York City Police Department is the largest police force in the entire United States, in charge of protecting all five boroughs.

Apart from being one of the oldest police departments, the NYPD also happens to be as large as some European Armies. The bold "mission statement" of the New York Police Department is to "enforce the laws, preserve the peace, reduce fear, and provide for a safe environment."

The NYPD employs a number of Special Services like the Harbor Patrol and Scuba Team that employs the brave officers for underwater work and evidence recovery. The investigative intelligence unit of the NYPD is one of the best in the world!

SAFEST CITY

The New York City Fire Department's motto is "New York's Bravest," and rightfully so. **Besides the traditional fire fighting equipment, the FDNY also employs boats, helicopters, and small aircrafts to help New Yorkers.**

Along with the high profile presence of both the FDNY and the NYPD is the invisible force of the FBI and the CIA that make the city safe.

Additional security measures in the city also include thousands of unseen security cameras, unmarked police vehicles, and private security guards. So inspite of what you may have seen in the movies and on TV, the truth is that New York is one of the safest places to be.

IN THE WORLD

As you walk on 47th Street in New York City you are greeted by the magnificent diamond-shaped street lamps that adorn this famous block known as the Diamond District.

Nearly ninety-five percent of diamonds that enter the United States pass through this neighborhood.

This area, also known as the "Diamond and Jewelry Way," is the world's largest shopping district for all sizes and shapes of diamonds and fine jewelry.

If you're shopping for world-class jewelry, or the perfect stone for the girl of your dreams, the Diamond District in the city is the place to be. As everyone knows, diamonds "are a girl's best friend!"

48

This era is also marked by a number of modern advancements. Milling became an important trade, and windmills dotted the horizon. In 1720, the first shipyard was built, bringing in a rise in the shipbuilding industry.

Then the printing press sparked a new revolution in the cultural landscape as New York began its first newspaper, called the *New York Gazette* in 1725. From then on, publishing grew as a big business, fostering a great growth of journalism, starting with the penny press and rising to the prominent newspapers of the modern day.

Art, theater, and education also saw a boost in this time with the establishment of the city's first theater as well as its first college, the King's College, now Columbia University.

For years, resentment against British rule had been building, and things got very tense when the Stamp Act was introduced in 1765, angering many New Yorkers who shut their businesses as a mark of protest.

By 1775, with the American Declaration of Independence, there began a full-blown armed conflict, and by 1781, the Continental Army had managed to force the British to surrender. Finally, Great Britain formally recognized US independence in 1783 at the Treaty of Paris, and the fighting ended.

continued on page 66

NEW YORK CITY
since 1664
HISTORY

The *New York Water Taxi* is a hop-on, hop-off sight-seeing ferry along the city's waterfront where you can explore Brooklyn and Manhattan at your own pace.

WATER TAXI

ROOSEVELT ISLAND

GOVERNORS

There are thirty-four obscure
islands in the New York City
area and four of the five
boroughs that make up the
city are islands or are
connected to an island!

Manhattan Island is the most known island in the world. Liberty Island and Ellis Island have historical significance where millions of immigrants passed through on their way to making a home in America.

New York City is located in one of the world's largest natural harbors with almost 600 miles of waterfront, making it a wonderful gateway for finance, transportation, and food distribution.

Staten Island and Roosevelt Island are wonderful places to live. Roosevelt Island is now a residential haven to many who work in Manhattan, using the air tramway as their means of transportation. Governors Island in the heart of the city harbor is a world of unique promises and holds historic significance in the American Revolutionary War.

ISLANDS ISLANDS ISLANDS

Pharmaceutical & Health Care

New York City is the leader in medical research and pharmaceutical manufacturing across the world, boasting some of the biggest names in these fields.

Top-class laboratories are engaged in cutting-edge research and innovation in all ailments, including cancer research, joint diseases, mental health research, and all the specialties.

We're changing how the world treats cancer.

1250

Memorial Sloan Kettering Cancer Center

It is no wonder, then, that patients needing emergency surgery and critical care are often flown in on helicopter ambulances for complex treatments in New York, such as highly specialized procedures for accidents and trauma.

New York hospitals have a flawless reputation as top-class institutions known for their professionalism, stellar care, and state-of-the-art facilities.

This attracts the world's top medical professionals, doctors, and surgeons to work in the city and rise in their careers. Students of medicine opt for residencies and training here, seeking the first-class education offered by New York City hospitals and schools, which are among the highest-ranked all across the world.

MOVIES, THEATER & MORE...

Before Hollywood sprouted up, New York City was the epicenter of movies and filmmaking. However, due to logistics and a milder climate, Hollywood soon exceeded NYC's production capabilities, becoming the well-known Tinsel Town. But New York is once again pushing Hollywood to the backseat by employing over 100,000 New Yorkers and bringing in a substantial amount to the city's economy.

Not only was New York the first choice for recent films such as Spider Man, The Great Gatsby, it has more than doubled its production of television shows and series in the last decade alone.

Measuring America's Might

Located in the city, the Intrepid Air and Space Museum is a true show of America's might as well as an awareness and educational show honoring the country's heroes. The Fighting "I," also known as USS *Intrepid* and is one of 24 Essex-class aircraft carriers built during World War II for the United States Navy.

She participated in several campaigns most notably the Battle of Leyte Gulf. Her notable achievements include being the recovery ship for a Mercury and a Gemini space mission.

New York
State of
Mind

EDUCATION IN THE BIG APPLE

The New York City Public School system has over 1.1 million students in more than 1,700 schools with a budget of nearly $25 billion making it the largest in the world.

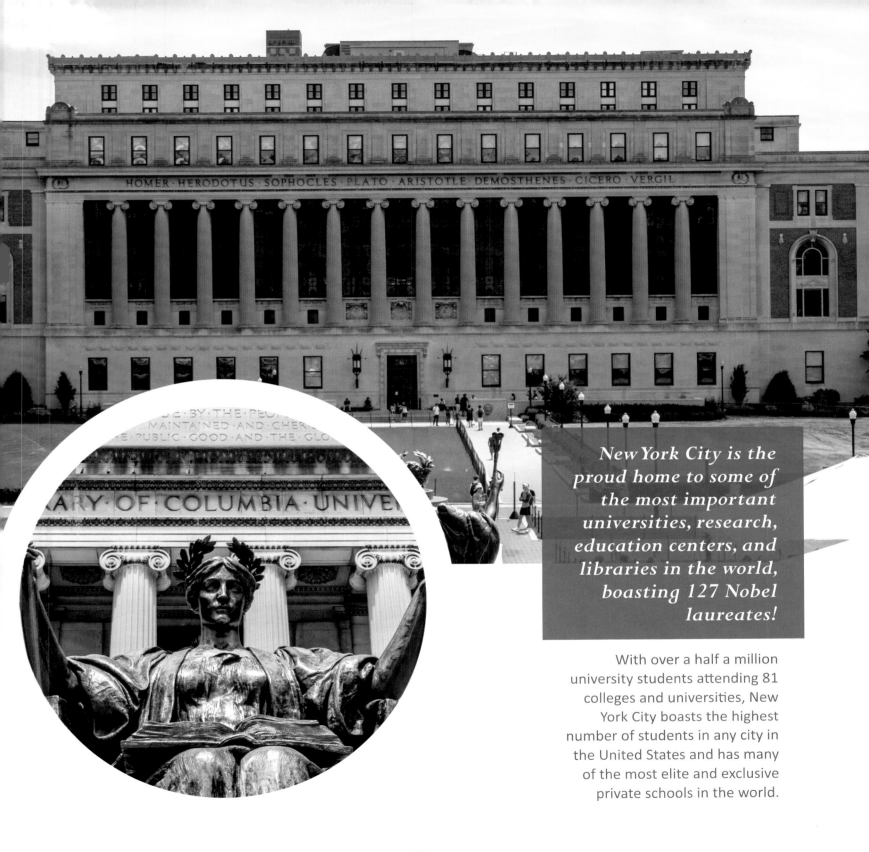

New York City is the proud home to some of the most important universities, research, education centers, and libraries in the world, boasting 127 Nobel laureates!

With over a half a million university students attending 81 colleges and universities, New York City boasts the highest number of students in any city in the United States and has many of the most elite and exclusive private schools in the world.

Spring in the city

As winter flows into spring, there are literally hundreds of things to do in New York City with the green foliage, cherry blossoms, and sparkling rivers as a beautiful backdrop to the City That Never Sleeps!

People from all walks of life celebrate spring in the city by heading to the numerous parks while taking in some sunshine, sipping chilled wine in the outdoor cafes, or paddling about in the quaint ponds at Central Park.

New York City in the spring is chock-full of activities too numerous to begin to name, but there is something for everyone during this blissful season!

HEALTH NUT CITY

Known as "The City That Never Sleeps," New York City could also be known as the "City of Fitness Freaks"!

It takes a lot of energy to keep up with the pulse of the city, and New Yorkers have proven that they are up to the task as they eagerly participate in literally hundreds of options to stay in shape!

One of the favorite fitness pastimes of New Yorkers is bicycling and jogging along the water in Battery Park City. There is bootcamp by the Hudson, or meditation in Battery Park. Some who live in high-rises never leave their buildings to work up a sweat, as there are state-of-the-art workout facilities just an elevator ride away!

New Yorkers also include the entire family for Kid's Fitness in Central Park as well as other family friendly workout sessions all year long. The fitness fanatics of New York aren't without options to keep up with the pace of their beloved city.

The first President of the United States of America, George Washington was inaugurated on April 30, 1789, in Federal Hall at New York City, where he took his presidential oath of office.

New York served as the first US capital from 1785 to 1790, during which time it began its recovery from war, a process that was sped up thanks to the city's flourishing cotton economy.

By 1810, New York had become one of the most important ports in the country. The growing cotton industry pushed for the construction of a better transport system linking the port city to the interior parts of the country, and so, the Erie Canal was created in 1825 to link the Hudson to the interiors.

At first the city grew haphazardly, but soon that was to change. Because by 1811, one of New York's most iconic features was established—its grid-like ordering of roads and avenues, slotted according to perfect, parallel lines. By 1820, New York was the country's largest city.

Traditionally reliant on wells and springs for their water needs, the city established the Croton Aqueduct to channel water from the Croton River with the help of gravity into reservoirs in Manhattan, laying the foundation for the development of the modern waterworks that crisscross under the city.

continued on page 74

NEW YORK CITY
since 1664
HISTORY

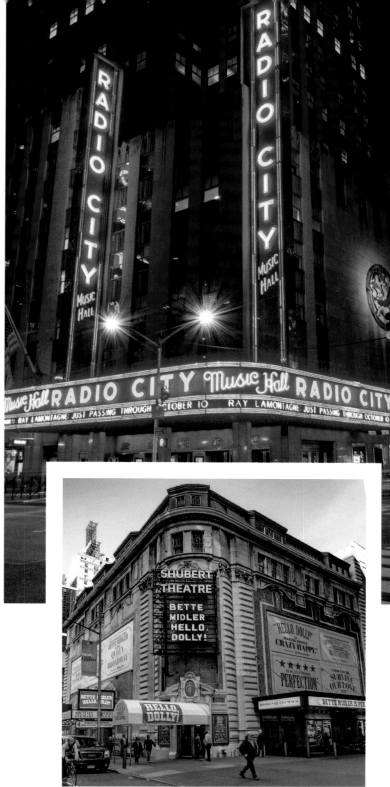

BROADWAY

With over 13 million people attending Broadway shows in Manhattan each year, NYC is the theater destination for tourists and New Yorkers alike!

NEW YORK CITY GOVERNMENT

Mayor

Bill de Blasio

|

Deputy Mayors

|

Commissioners

|

Borough Presidents

|

Councilmen

51 Council members

The governing body of New York City is headquartered at City Hall in Lower Manhattan. The annual budget in the year 2019 was over $89 billion and employs over 200,000 people.

Christmas cheer!

There's no doubt—the most magical time in New York is Christmastime! The choirs sing hymns and carols that fill the streets, where lovers stroll hand in hand and turn to each other with smiles and kisses.

Decked in the Christmas colors of green, red, and gold, the city transforms into a wonderland of twinkling lights and dazzling decorations. People adorn their homes with Christmas trees, holly, and mistletoe, while shops fill their brightly lit holiday windows with creative displays.

The enormous Rockefeller Center Christmas Tree draws thousands of spectators. In the ice rinks, children giggle with glee and spin circles on their skates. The church bells chime, drawing reunited families.

Like magic dust, the snowflakes drifting down bring smiles and cheer to every heart.

Mothers clasp the hands of their children and fathers hoist the little ones onto their shoulders to show them the beautiful sights.

As street musicians regale the crowds, children run and play in the snow, and the city takes on the glow of a magical winter wonderland.

It's hard to miss Santa Claus, as you find him everywhere! From street corners waving to the kids, to pedaling rickshaws and giving out rides, to greeting folks and taking selfies.

Shops and street vendors spill out all manner of assortments of Christmas goodies, jewelry, hats, and scarves. Bright lights reveal flushed faces, joyous eyes, and wondrous revelers dressed in beautiful outfits, exchanging greetings and easy smiles.

As the countdown to Christmas approaches, the mayhem and fervor increases. Suddenly everyone rushes to complete their last-minute shopping activities, clogging the roads and mall aisles with their vehicles and shopping carts. But even when they collide, they smile and say, "Merry Christmas!"

Surely, Christmastime in New York City is the merriest, cheeriest, prettiest time! So let it draw you, warm your heart like old wine, and touch your heart with the Christmas spirit.

The second half of the 19th century witnessed exponential growth. Horse-drawn streetcars began to plow; streets began to be cobbled, starting with Stone Street. Broadway was fashioned out of parts of a Native Indian walking trail. Immigrants continued to flow in, settling in distinct ethnic neighborhoods where they established their own churches, schools, and social clubs.

The *New York Times* began circulation in 1851. Many of the city's most prominent features were established around this time, with the New York Police Department in 1845.

Emphasis was laid on developing public parks, and in 1858 Central Park was born, with Prospect Park in Brooklyn following in 1867.

In 1878 came the first telephone lines, and quickly following in their footsteps came electricity in the 1880s, beginning to light up the growing skyscrapers that we see today.

This was also a time where feats of great modern civil engineering were witnessed, as the longest suspension bridges ever seen by the city were constructed, starting with the Brooklyn Bridge in 1883. These bridges still attract millions of visitors every year.

continued on page 84

The City of Libraries

Without a doubt the most famous of the libraries is the iconic New York Public Library situated on Fifth Avenue. Crystal chandeliers adorn the Rose Reading Room, inspiring all who enter to enjoy over fifty million reading and educational items.

The libraries in the New York area are some of the most beautiful examples of architecture in the entire world, and there are plenty of options to choose from for your literary endeavors!

75

Many highly educated individuals make their home in this fast-paced metropolis, flocking to major industries from finance, technology, fashion, IT, medicine, and law to media and business.

These aspiring women and men draw paychecks as high as six figures. With razor-sharp focus on excelling in every aspect of their work, grabbing opportunities for growth, and amassing wealth, these young dreamers' hard work also puts money back into the city's growing economy.

As work can stretch into as many as 14 hours a day, these young folks also know how to live it up and party hard. They rock the hippest locales around the city during the week and get away to their weekend beach homes on picturesque locations in coveted towns.

City of the young

New York City teems with spectacular opportunities that attract ambitious young millennials from across the world.

Queens

With over 2.3 million residents from 130 countries,

Queens is geographically the largest of all boroughs and is known as the most ethnically diverse urban area in the entire world. Historically a collection of small villages founded by the Dutch in the 1680s, Queens has grown in both commercial and residential prominence.

It is home to the New York Mets and host of the US Open Tennis Tournament. The airspace above Queens is the most congested in all of America, transporting passengers both domestic and international every day!

Sixth Avenue was renamed "Avenue of the Americas" in 1945 by the New York City Council to honor Pan-American ideals and principles and to encourage both Central and South America to build consulates along the avenue. This nearly four-mile stretch of Sixth Avenue is adorned with the Coat of Arms with both South & Central American countries on either sides.

Avenue of the Americas

The Garment District, also know to the world as the Fashion District, is located in a stretch of Midtown Manhattan. It is home to numerous major fashion labels, showrooms, design production, and wholesale selling! Since the early 20th century, this area has been known as the center for fashion manufacturing and design in the world!

FASHION WALK *of* FAME

Fashion Walk of Fame celebrates excellence in American design by honoring the New York designers who have had a significant and lasting impact on the way the world dresses.

New York has been the undisputed center of American fashion since the mid-19th Century when the development of mass-production led to the growth of the apparel trades. The birth of the Fashion District, also known as the Garment Center, occurred in the 1920s, when a large group of garment manufacturers relocated to Seventh Avenue. New loft space was developed especially to accommodate "modern" manufacturing and to satisfy labor's demands for safer working conditions. By 1931, this District had the largest concentration of apparel manufacturers in the world and since then has been home to the greatest names in American design.

A project of The Fashion Center Business Improvement District.

Established 1999

FLOWER SHOWS

When visiting New York City, don't forget to "stop and smell the roses" at one of the many flower shows during the warmer seasons! Among the most well-known annual flower shows is the Macy's Flower Show in the iconic department store during the month of April.

Head to the Bronx to experience the New York Botanical Garden founded in 1891 and now a National Historic Landmark. This is one of the greatest botanical gardens in the entire world and the largest in the United States, known for its diverse landscape and extensive collections and gardens.

One of the most dazzling shows at the New York Botanical Garden is the annual Orchid Show, designed by the world's leading floral designers.

Though New York City entertains all
four seasons, Autumn is definitely one of
the most beautiful and activity-filled
times to visit this vibrant city!
As the leaves begin to change, bursting
with vibrant-colored trees, there are
many gardens and parks to be explored
to view this magnificent sight!

Because New York was such an important port, it drew people of all backgrounds and calibers, and in these coming decades, the city also began to be a center of great cultural and artistic development, sprouting up cultural centers, museums, and theaters that in turn played a role in attracting more talent.

The MET opened in 1870, Carnegie Hall in 1891, the Museum of Natural History in 1869. The Met Opera House opened its doors in 1883, and Broadway witnessed such a quick series of openings of new theaters that soon the term Broadway came to mean a certain kind of theater.

In 1886, the French gifted the United States the Statue of Liberty and it was installed in New York Harbor.

And so, toward the end of the century, New York had begun to shape into the city we now know. The five boroughs voted to consolidate with Manhattan in 1895, forming the five-borough Greater New York.

This period was also one of great turmoil that ultimately brought an end to slavery. New York was no stranger to these movements and had enacted the Gradual Emancipation Act in 1799, a series of laws that incrementally freed slaves. By the time the 1840 census was taken, there were no slaves in the city.

However, in the 1860 presidential elections, Republicans under Lincoln supported the banning of slavery in US territories, against which the southern states rebelled.

continued on page 94

"Flea" the city!

The five boroughs of the city have some of the best flea markets both indoors and out, with everything from furniture to clothes, to jewelry, and more!

During the summer season the city is busy with street fairs giving a taste of various cuisines prepared fresh in front of you, trendy clothes, indoor and outdoor plants, jewelry, and much more.

It's
FUN
for all!

The Bronx Zoo is one of the largest zoos in the world with more than 6,000 animals, the Bug Carousel, camel rides, and other activities!
Plan to spend a full day at the Bronx Zoo since there are so many things to see and fun things to do!

There is no shortage of fun for kids of all ages at New York's Zoos and Aquarium with a zoo in every borough and one of the best aquariums, with loads of activities for all who visit!

The Central Park Zoo is probably the most famous where kids and parents alike not only enjoy the "picture book zoo," but they can also take in the incredible sights of Manhattan!

Coney Island is home to the oldest operating aquarium in the United States with some amazing underwater viewing tanks and a state-of-the-art Aqua Theater with Sea Lion Celebration shows and a new 3-D theater for seriously cool entertainment for the whole family.

The glorious George Washington Bridge is one of the oldest bridges connecting Manhattan to the rest of the United States. It was named after the First President, George Washington, who was sworn into the city office.

Spanning the Hudson River between Manhattan and New Jersey, the GWB is the main artery of commerce and trade to New York City, connecting millions of people.

This beautiful double-decker suspension bridge was hailed as a marvel of engineering when it was built. It spans across a hefty 2.5 miles in length, providing eight lanes for vehicles. Stretching across the roaring river under glorious skies, the bridge is a breathtaking sight.

In New York City, you can buy your dreams! No matter what you desire, this city is definitely going to satisfy you!

Every shopper's haven

From the glitz and glitter of luxury goods to the humbler artisanal or thrift-store treasures, New York City offers an endless array of delights. It's no wonder, then, that it's known as the shopping paradise of the world!

So famous is New York for its shopping splendor that tourists pour into the city in the millions, aiming primarily to shop.

Filled with trendy boutiques, prime-vintage collections, resplendent indoor malls, avant-garde galleries, and chain stores with designer merchandise.

From Madison Avenue to Lexington, to the many underground malls, New York City is an ever-flowing carnival of the senses when it comes to shopping.

New York City is where the most famous brands in the world come together, as though nature's bounty had burst open in the form of anything and everything one could dream.

New York is one of the busiest cities in the world! Thus, to support its millions of small and large ventures, the shipping and delivery industry plays a major role.

Not just shipping!

From delivery bikes, to walkers, to vans and trucks plowing roadways and highways, to cargo ships sailing to the harbors—so many operations are solely dedicated to the act of moving goods and services around.

Airports around the city offer essential international shipping and cargo transportation services, while special ocean freight and stevedoevring centers help move heavy building equipment.

Competitive services offer package-pickup from doorstep while assuring same day delivery. As every borough teams up with USPS, UPS, and Fed Ex centers, they cement their reliable network with the rest of the country and abroad.

NYC Harbor

The stunning New York Harbor is one of the largest natural harbors of the world. This gateway between the world and US has played a historic role in the rise of New York City as one of the most important hubs of the world.

Even to this day, New York Harbor welcomes over 5,000 ships a year from across the globe, thus acting as a key source for goods, food, and fuel in the country. Nearly a third of imports to the US pass through this harbor!

It was largely due to the harbor that the city grew to its present epic proportions and became what it is today, thriving from being one of the most important international frontiers for the entire world.

African Americans living in the southern states then joined "The Great Migration" moving up north. "For those who landed in the hotbed of Harlem," wrote historian Laban Carrick Hill, "it was a time of intellectual, artistic, literary, and political blossoming."

Even though the Prohibition was on, the speakeasies and night-clubs of Harlem drew crowds, and Broadway musicals like *Hot Chocolate* and plays like *Harlem* opened to packed houses. In this climate then, there was a boom in literature, art, and music, and a great spurt in blues and jazz.

The early years of the 20th century bore witness to the growth of some of the world's most stunning modern architecture. The Flatiron building was built in 1902, and at 21 stories high, it was the city's first skyscraper.

Its angular architecture resembled an iron press, and hence the name. In 1904, New York's first subway line began operations. The New York Public Library was built in 1911, Grand Central in 1913. The Chrysler building, built in 1930, was the first building in the world to break the 300-meter barrier, followed by the Empire State building in 1931, which once again broke the world record for the tallest building.

continued on page 104

NEW YORK CITY
since 1664
HISTORY

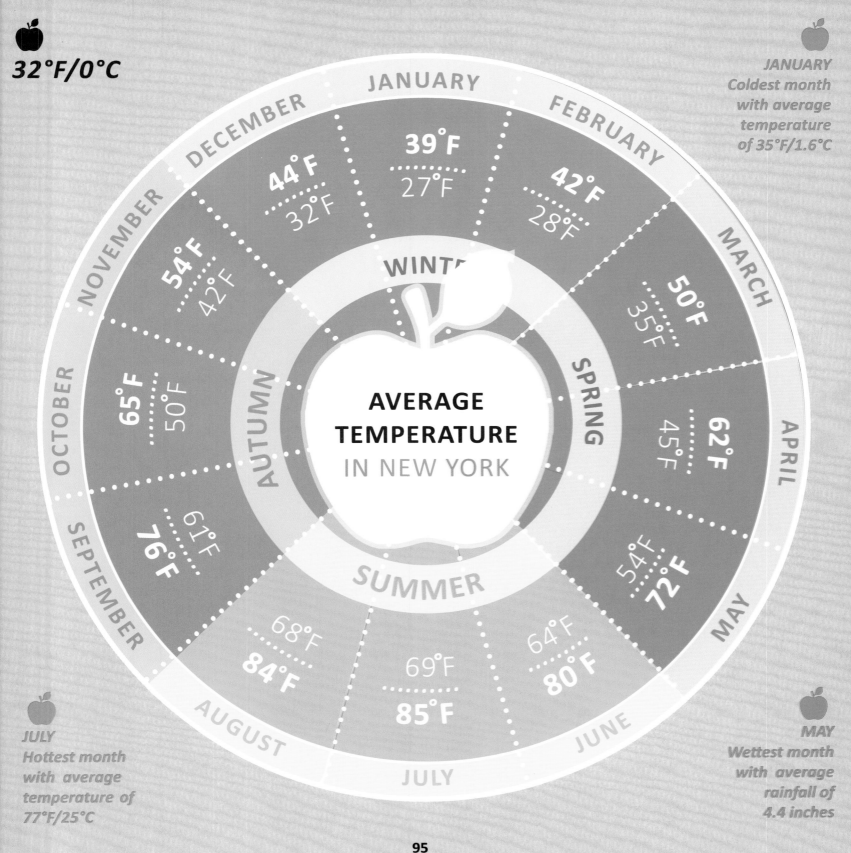

32°F/0°C

AVERAGE
TEMPERATURE
IN NEW YORK

JANUARY
Coldest month with average temperature of 35°F/1.6°C

JULY
Hottest month with average temperature of 77°F/25°C

MAY
Wettest month with average rainfall of 4.4 inches

JANUARY 39°F 27°F
FEBRUARY 42°F 28°F
MARCH 50°F 35°F
APRIL 62°F 45°F
MAY 72°F 54°F
JUNE 80°F 64°F
JULY 85°F 69°F
AUGUST 84°F 68°F
SEPTEMBER 76°F 61°F
OCTOBER 65°F 50°F
NOVEMBER 54°F 42°F
DECEMBER 44°F 32°F

WINTER
SPRING
SUMMER
AUTUMN

NYC

FASHION
2020

New York City is considered the
fashion capital of the world, with
over 900 fashion companies headquartered
in the city that generate more than
fifteen billion dollars in annual sales!
The many showrooms and fashion
shows attract more than half a million
visitors to NYC each year, and New
York City's famous Fashion Weeks
that are held in February and
September bring in close to $900
million to the city's economy alone!

TOP-NOTCH CONVENTION CENTERS

Each year, millions of connoisseurs gravitate to New York City for its countless spectacular expos, conventions, markets, and trade fairs.

They come from far and wide, not only from the United States but from all over. This city hosts some of the most important conventions in the world!

For people interested in a variety of niche fields, these impactful, futuristic trade fairs have become vital and significant events.

The convention centers in the city are colossal and magnificent. Featuring acres and acres of space for halls, performance areas, conference rooms, booths and more, these venues—like the Javits Center and the Madison Square Garden Expo Center—play a key role in leading the world in setting trends and benchmarks, and predicting the future.

FOOD LOVERS
Paradise

From quickly grabbing a juicy burger or steaming slice of pizza, to savoring your favorite caviar on toast points during a lavish seven-course meal, there is simply no end to the delicious choices in the New York City area!

To simply say that New York City has wonderful food would be an understatement. The fact of the matter is, New York is a food lovers' paradise! Because of the multicultural and financial diversity of this great city, there are literally thousands of delicious foods and culinary treats to sample, twenty-four hours a day.

It is said that there are enough restaurants in New York City for one person to eat out every night for 65 years, and never visit the same place twice!

From Greenwich Village to Chelsea, from Brooklyn to the Upper West Side, there is a never-ending wonderland of fabulous foods to be tasted and memorable fun to be had! So, grab a hot dog in Central Park or crunch into a delicious cannoli in Little Italy!

TRUMP TOWER

The New York "White House"

The father of our country, George Washington, was sworn in as the first president of the United States in New York City not far from where Donald Trump, the 45th president of the United States was born and raised!

Prior to becoming president, Donald Trump, a prominent New York City real estate developer and businessman, began planning the development of the 664-foot-high tower between 56th and 57th Streets in Midtown Manhattan.

Art and more

An inspiration for every artist, the art galleries and auction houses in the city are among the main attractions for millions of tourists every year, giving visitors a visually stunning experience they will never forget!

From Fifth Avenue to Soho, east to west, there is art everywhere to explore. These venues feature huge colorful advertisements, paintings, sculptures, beautiful wall murals and the work of local and international artists.

For 85 years, New York held the title for having the tallest skyscrapers in the world.

By the early 20th century, New York became a leading business center in the world as it served as the headquarters of more than two-thirds of the top 100 American corporations.

A breathtaking rise in public transportation came about, where several old Indian trails were fortified, and water transport was developed with the building of canals like Erie and Gowanus, the rise of steamboats traveling from the New York harbor to other Hudson and coastal ports. Rapid transit began to develop with the establishment of the Interborough Rapid Transit Company (IRT) and elevated railway tracks began to appear around the city.

In the 1920s, motor cars began to hit the road, with the first automobile launched by Ford called the Model T.

The building of modern roads along with these fast moving cars gave young people more mobility and freedom, so they could go where they pleased, and dancing, jazz, musicals, and theater all saw a surge in popularity and attendance. New York's aerospace engineering industry also grew rapidly, and it is today one of the top ten in the country for aircraft manufacturing.

continued on page 114

NEW YORK CITY
since 1664
HISTORY

The history of Chinese people in New York began during the 1800s and in 1870 Chinatown was established in the city. Today there are close to six hundred thousand Chinese people in New York City alone. The iconic Chinatown in Lower Manhattan is just one of nine Chinatown neighborhoods in the five boroughs, and contains the largest ethnic Chinese population! Another "Chinatown" to explore is located in Flushing, Queens, just minutes by train from Midtown Manhattan.

Miles & miles of

beaches

Surrounding the city of New York with its extensive coastline are miles of beaches filled with surf and sand where New Yorkers flock to beat the summer heat!

Some of the beaches closest to New York City are Rockaway beach with its famous boardwalk, markets, and outdoor activities, and Coney Island with three miles of sandy beaches and iconic amusement parks.

PENN STATION

With a footfall of nearly half a million commuters each day, New York City's Penn Station is the busiest station across North America. Ensconced in beautifully covered architecture, the station connects New York to several important cities by rail. To provide its passengers with a safe and comfortable travel experience, Penn Station boasts of several wonderful facilities selling meals, coffee, fresh squeezed juices, and wholesome food.

The New York Vibe
when workaholics chill!

The annual New York City Marathon is the largest marathon in the world, with close to 100,000 applicants per year and nearly two million spectators lining the course as runners pass through all five boroughs, finishing the race in NYC's Central Park! Beginning on Staten Island near the Verrazzano-Narrows Bridge, the runners use both sides of the upper level of the bridge and the westbound side of the lower level. The dramatic sight of the bridge filled with runners in the opening minutes of the race is one of the most memorable visions of the entire race.

The runners then tour through Brooklyn, passing through a variety of neighborhoods.

Toward the end of the marathon, the runners go south through Harlem down Fifth Avenue and then into Central Park where thousands of well-wishers and spectators cheer them on during the last mile.

TO THE DEFENDERS OF THE UNION 1861 1865

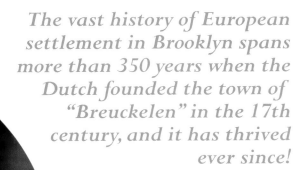

The vast history of European settlement in Brooklyn spans more than 350 years when the Dutch founded the town of "Breuckelen" in the 17th century, and it has thrived ever since!

After the American Revolution, the waterfront site of Brooklyn was used to build merchant vessels and in 1806 became an active US Navy Shipyard.

The Brooklyn Navy Yard was responsible for building war ships for the United States Navy. The amazing efforts of its workers during WWII helped tremendously for the United States involvement with the war.

Famous for Coney Island, the Brooklyn Museum, and the Barclays Center, Brooklyn is a great destination for fun.

America's Industrial Might

The Brooklyn Navy Yard was a huge, 200-mile campus, building ships for the Second World War, and several sites around Brooklyn, like the site now occupied by Ikea, were once ship-docking yards. The "roaring twenties" was an era of dramatic social and political change. For the first time ever, more Americans lived in cities than farms, and the nation's wealth more than doubled, pushing Americans to a more affluent "consumer society."

This period was also one where women's empowerment grew by leaps and bounds, and the flapper became a symbol of an empowered, progressive woman.

1920 was a landmark year for the rise of women's empowerment, as the 19th Amendment gave women the right to vote and they cast their ballots for the first time in US history in the fall presidential elections, paving the way for more growth to come.

When the First World War started, women began to take on new responsibilities in the war effort as men were drafted and sent to war. They formed the Motor Corps of America, running transportation and ambulatory services for military personnel. They formed knitting circles to knit wool for the needs of the soldiers.

After the Second World War, the interstate highways prompted wealthier people to begin moving out to the slowly upcoming suburbs, and changes began to occur around the city, with diminishing public services and a lowered tax base.

continued on page 124

THE CITY OF MUSEUMS

Explore the art, culture, music, history, and more in one of the hundreds of museums in New York City! From the more well-known establishments to the obscure galleries, there is more than enough to choose from for art lovers from all parts of the globe!

The largest art museum in the United States is the iconic Metropolitan Museum of Art, with 400 galleries.

Boats and Cruises on the New York Harbor

Because Manhattan is an island, there are many opportunities to view its surroundings by water, whether by ferry, water taxi, or a midnight cruise! For a relaxing dinner cruise with a view, there are many options available where visitors can bask in the glow of the setting sun and harbor lights! Dinner cruises around New York City can be two to three hours, or all night extravaganzas, depending on your taste!

If there was ever a trophy for sports-crazy cities, New York would surely be in the running for the top prize.

New York hosts some of the biggest sporting events in the world. Events so extraordinary they are the envy of everyone. New York has produced some of the finest sports teams, leading the games from baseball, basketball, football, soccer, ice hockey, and tennis to rugby.

This obsession for sports unites New Yorkers, bridging differences, helping people find common ground for gathering together in celebration and joy, finding their spirits uplifted and united.

Sports tournaments animate crowds to the tune of millions, drawing out not only all the sports-crazy fans but also thousands of sports-hungry tourists!

There is nothing fans haven't done here, from decking their homes and cars to storming the courts, from streaking stark naked across the fields to stripping shirtless in sub-zero temperatures!

118

HORSE RACING

Included among the many hobbies and pastimes of New Yorkers is the passion for thoroughbred horse racing which draws tens of thousands of fans each year!

Horse racing events allow for natives and tourists alike to experience the thrill of watching the world's best jockeys and thoroughbred horses vie for the championship title!

Built in 1894, Aqueduct Racetrack in Queens is the only racetrack located within New York City limits and it is the headquarters for the New York Racing Association.

One of the most iconic and widely known images in the world is the logo

Belonging to the State of New York it was created to promote the city. Designed by Milton Glaser, this beloved logo was made in 1977 to promote New York state during the turbulent 1970s.

The Fourth of July Holiday is a day of resplendent celebrations in the city!

4th of July

It marks the anniversary of the Declaration of Independence in 1776.

New York City was the first capital, and to this date, it hosts the biggest celebrations and the largest fireworks display across the country. When America became a free country George Washington became its first president.

In the evening right after sundown starts the spectacle that everyone has been waiting for!

The skies split into the most dazzling pyrotechnics of gorgeous light and color. The entire horizon above the East River comes alive with fireworks that go off lighting up the skyline and reflecting in the river.

123

This period came to be known as "white flight" or "out migration." To counter this flow, the government passed the Nationality Act in 1965 to promote immigration to the United States, where the incoming immigrant populations revitalized the neighborhoods and the economy.

These decades also saw a lot of fascinating cultural and artistic developments, such as the Olympic Games that were hosted by the city in 1932, the Woodstock festival of 1969, and the burgeoning of financial institutions and businesses.

Times Square was named after the *New York Times*, whose offices had relocated there in 1904.

While New York had always been one of the most prominent centers of trade, toward the 1990s it also became the largest port in the world. In 1952, the United Nations established their headquarters in the city. Soon, New York rose to the status of the world's premier financial center and home to the New York Stock Exchange and NASDAQ, the two largest stock exchanges in the world.

The New York Stock Exchange is the world's largest stock exchange by dollar volume.

continued on page 134

NEW YORK CITY
since 1664
HISTORY

Within the five boroughs of New York City there are more than 1,700 parks with playgrounds attracting millions of people every year!

In the middle of Manhattan is the iconic Central Park, one of the most famous parks in the entire world! Named a historic landmark in 1962, it is also the most visited urban park in the United States and one of the most filmed locations across the globe!

bustling NIGHTLIFE

New York City at night is just as lively as the daytime, perhaps even more so!

As the sun sets, the city turns into a party-lover's dream come true, offering adrenaline-filled adventures through dance clubs, pubs, burlesque and striptease joints, and more.

Glittering, buzzing, bustling, the city turns into a fiesta of the senses, regaling folks with jazz, blues, rock, and hip-hop all night long. Mouthwatering, delectable delights are served in all-night cafes.

Young people hop from bar to bar, trying all the beers on tap or swigging away shots of tequila. Lovers of dancing and singing can hit open-mic karaoke bars, moving with the beats and singing away their blues.

Hidden underground speakeasies and joints usher visitors into their dark bellies. People visit gay or queer bars to meet other people and get their favorite drinks.

The city takes its nightlife so seriously that it actually appointed a Nightlife Mayor. Now, if that doesn't spell fun, then what does?

All-night shopping centers around Times Square draw excited shoppers and tourists till the wee hours of the morning. Bars and pubs throw open their doors to spill soft light and music onto the sidewalks, where drunken revelers traipse all night long in groups and pairs, drunk on the most daring cocktails and more. The bartenders in New York are famous for their mixological skills, making everything from martinis to absinthe.

Many water taxis and ferries provide an important link, of which several are free services for the public. The skies above New York City are always criss crossed with vital air routes where commercial and private airplanes and helicopters operate.

As cars thunder down New York highways, subways cut miles underground, ferries dock in harbors, and buses plow—through the crowded streets—the mass transit system in New York City is fondly referred to as the life blood of the city.

With its extensive, inexpensive, and reliable public transportation system, New York stands unique among all other US cities. In fact, the mass transit system is so committed to service that it operates its subways 24 hours a day, 365 days a year, come hail or snow!

New York has 34 subway lines with over 469 stops and over 800 miles of track, connecting all the major hubs in the 5 boroughs.

**Roadway
Highway
Skyway
Expressway
Waterway**

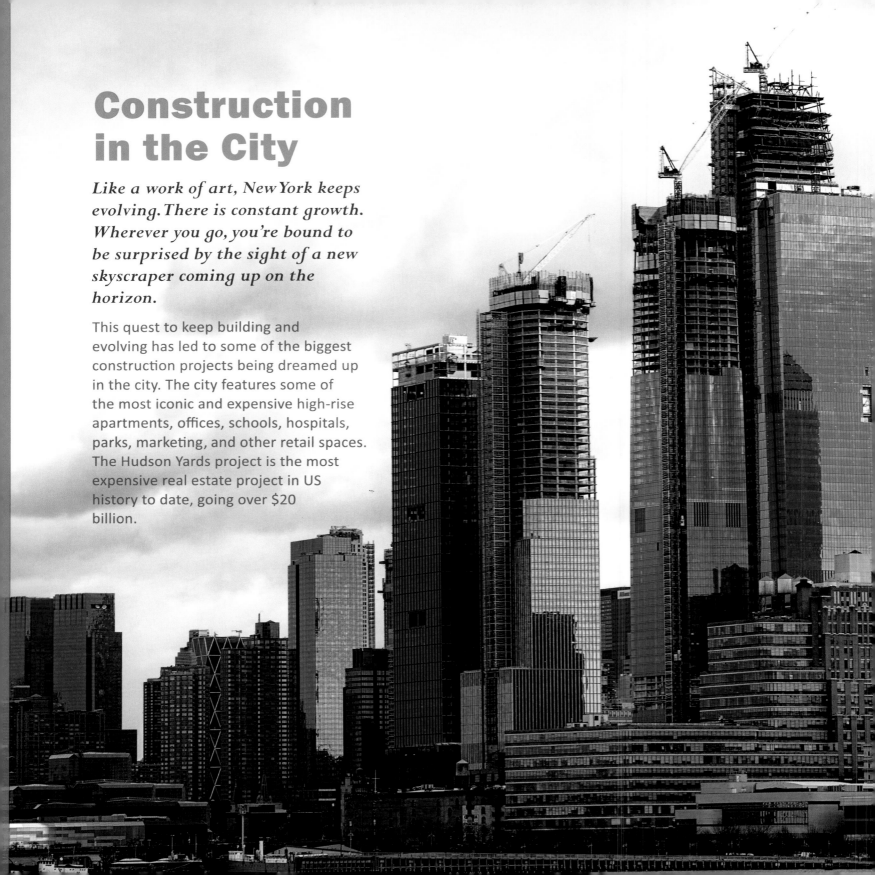

Construction in the City

Like a work of art, New York keeps evolving. There is constant growth. Wherever you go, you're bound to be surprised by the sight of a new skyscraper coming up on the horizon.

This quest to keep building and evolving has led to some of the biggest construction projects being dreamed up in the city. The city features some of the most iconic and expensive high-rise apartments, offices, schools, hospitals, parks, marketing, and other retail spaces. The Hudson Yards project is the most expensive real estate project in US history to date, going over $20 billion.

If there's one constant in New York City, it's the ubiquity of change! The breathtaking skylines of the city offer a dose of inspiration and awe to visitors and residents alike.

The highest safety standards are adhered to, and at present, construction workers are earning the highest wages.

The fascinating designs of the buildings and the mirror-like skyscrapers reaching for the stars are a reflection of the spirit and zeal of the city.

Love Is in the Air

ROOFTOP FARMING

New York City is a new leader in rooftop agriculture and this innovative commercial endeavor is expected to continue to expand rapidly in the near future!

Gotham Greens in the Greenpoint section of Brooklyn began harvesting from its hydroponic rooftop greenhouse in 2011 and has spread its operation to Queens and the Bronx employing "rooftop farmers." The Brooklyn Grange proudly farms at the Brooklyn Navy Yard with rows of squash, scallions, and beefsteak tomatoes.

Manhattan is also the leading center in the US for banking, finance, and communication, as well as a leading center for technology, real estate, insurance, health care, communications, mass media, journalism, publishing, and creative industries like fashion, design, architecture, theater and film.

At present, New York is home to 8,550,405 residents according to a July 2015 census report, and is the most populous US city. Three million of its residents are foreign born, making it part of the top ten cosmopolitan cities around the world.

Over 200 languages are spoken here, but according to the *New York Times*, some experts believe this number is closer to 800.

The greatest city in the world, New York

The sleek architecture of the Oculus lends a different vision of what a transportation hub should be.

Though New York City is home to Grand Central Station as well as Penn Station at Madison Square Garden, the Oculus, designed by acclaimed architect Santiago Calatrava, is the centerpiece of the World Trade Center Transportation Hub.

Serving over 200,000 daily commuters as well as millions of annual visitors from around the world, its state-of-the-art integrated pedestrian network is the focal point of lower Manhattan.

The Oculus is the most upscale and modern underground network linking the city.

With multilevel dining and retail services, boasting concourses and a shoppers paradise as well, it is a must visit!

It's commonly remarked that ninety percent of what the world reads is written in New York City!

While we may chuckle at that, there's obviously great truth in the statement. Consider the attraction of New York City to the intellectuals of the world: as the city is so richly populated with world-class institutions, research labs, state-of-the-art hospitals, media houses, and art and history museums, the city draws to itself the best minds in each field like honey attracts bees.

In some ways, you can consider New York City to be the brain of the world. Now, the city boasts some of the best institutions of education, such as the Ivy League Columbia University and New York University.

Also thriving here are exclusive clubs from prestigious universities like Harvard, Princeton, and Yale, admitting only the most well known biologists, mathematicians, scientists, and intellectuals, who inform the fabric of the city. Famous for its intellectual life, you can feel the buzz of the New York brain when you step into the city. Come and get electrified!

*New York
Intellectuals*

The resilient New Yorkers

Stepping out of taxis! Crossing the streets, catching subway rides, waiting in line for coffee! No matter where you look, New York City is always bustling with people.

Fast, focused, driven, New Yorkers are among the most resilient and ambitious people across the world.

With over 20 million residents including the greater New York area it is the most populous city in the country. Mixing in New York like colors on a palette, people from hundreds of different countries live here, resulting in the most diverse city, with nearly 800 different languages spoken.

There is no shortage of spectacular parades in the Big Apple to celebrate the city's diversity and many cultures, and these celebrations draw millions of people year after year.

PARADES in the Big Apple

The Greenwich Village Halloween Parade is the nation's largest public Halloween celebration and has been a New York institution for almost 40 years making it an event not to miss!

The annual LGBT Pride March which takes place every June is one of the most colorful parades of all time and is one of the most cherished events of the New York Gay Pride Week festivities!

A tradition since the Civil War days, the NYC Easter Parade features all of the elaborate Easter finery and some of the most wonderful children's costumes you'll ever see!

Easter Parade

St. Patrick's Day

Perhaps the only New York parade that features leprechauns drinking green beer is the St. Patrick's Day parade which was originally organized in 1762 by Irish soldiers and is a great excuse to "party"!

New York City is definitely a cyclist friendly city, constantly making efforts to support more biking activities, arranging touring events, races, and awareness campaigns all around biking.

Now, the city has also rolled out millions of commuter bikes through the Citi Bike system, one of the largest user-friendly and eco-conscious bike sharing platforms for commuters in the world.

Thanks to the availability of these bikes, New York City has experienced a further drop in not only its air pollution, but also its bikers' weight! Not only is biking super-duper fun, but it's also great for the planet!

To New Yorkers
BIKING IS SEXY

Whether for commuting to work or training to compete in racing events, zealous and daring bikers can be spotted zipping across the city, sporting their designer helmets and chiseled calf-muscles.

City bikers deck their bikes with racing paraphernalia, lights, and custom paint jobs, while also installing baskets and child seats not only for their groceries and kids but also their dogs and cats!

Feeding the city!

New York City is fortunate to be located just south of an expanse of some of the largest, most fertile farmlands in New York state.

This puts the city in the prime position of being a food haven and sanctuary. Wonderful, fresh, beautiful produce is brought into the city all year round, transported on trucks through highways that link up in a crisscrossing and highly evolved network.

Other produce and products are exported around the harbor, bringing millions of tons of essential goods via cargo ships or air and land systems.

This places New York in the enviable position of being a center of food and drink. In this melting pot of hundreds of different cultures, many creative, innovative, and lip-smacking dishes have sprung up, produced and distributed through the thousands of multicultural kitchens around the city.

What many people don't know is that deep under the city of New York, there is a secret underbelly of mysterious and unbelievable places both magically, fascinatingly beautiful and downright scary and dangerous.

In the ground below NYC have sprouted many exquisite and world-class food joints, bars, and shopping arcades. Countless exciting adventures await in the caverns of the city's underbelly from illegal speakeasies to beer breweries, cheese factories, and museum galleries operating completely from under the earth.

Ensconced among the world's largest utility, water, and transportation systems of the world, this secret upside-down city of New York extends to depths as astonishing as 180 feet!

For the daring explorer, underground New York City offers a breadth of dreamy and hair-raising adventures. From the shadow catacombs under St. Patrick's Church, to crypts, pool tunnels, and the graffiti covered Freedom Tunnels, these underground spaces are the stuff of lore and legend!

Enter at your own peril, the shadows warn.

The city under ground

SEE YOU IN

NEW YORK

Notes

Notes